LOCOMOTIVE CATHEDRAL

BRANDEL FRANCE DE BRAVO

The Backwaters Press
An imprint of the University of Nebraska Press

© 2025 by the Board of Regents of the University of Nebraska

"Although the wind" from THE INK DARK MOON: LOVE POEMS BY ONO NO KOMACHI AND IZUMI SHIKIBU, WOMEN OF THE ANCIENT COURT OF JAPAN translated by Jane Hirshfield with Mariko Aratani, translation copyright © 1986, 1987, 1988, 1989, 1990 by Jane Hirshfield. Used by permission of Vintage Books, an imprint of the Knopf Doubleday Publishing Group, a division of Penguin Random House LLC.

"Although the wind" from *The Ink Dark Moon* by Ono no Komachi and Izumi Shikibu, published by Vintage Digital. Copyright © 1986, 1987, 1988, 1989, 1990 by Jane Hirshfield. Reprinted by permission of Penguin Books Limited.

"Bird Wings" from *The Essential Rumi*, translated by Coleman Barks, is used by permission of Coleman Barks.

Acknowledgments for the use of copyrighted material appear on pages 87–90, which constitute an extension of the copyright page.

All rights reserved. The Backwaters Press is an imprint of the University of Nebraska Press.

Library of Congress Cataloging-in-Publication Data
Names: France de Bravo, Brandel, author.
Title: Locomotive cathedral / Brandel France de Bravo.
Description: Lincoln: The Backwaters Press, an imprint of the University of Nebraska Press, 2025. | Series: The Backwaters Prize in Poetry honorable mention
Identifiers: LCCN 2024028324
ISBN 9781496240088 (paperback)
ISBN 9781496242464 (epub)
ISBN 9781496242471 (pdf)
Subjects: BISAC: POETRY / Women Authors | LCGFT: Poetry.
Classification: LCC PS3606.R36425 L63 2025 | DDC 811/.6—dc23/eng/20240628
LC record available at https://lccn.loc.gov/2024028324

Designed and set in Garamond Premier Pro by Lacey Losh.

"Kinetic and spectral, wise and suspicious of wisdom, Brandel France de Bravo's *Locomotive Cathedral* chugs into an expansive, vaulted space, where 'any raised surface can be an altar,' via a hybrid text of poems, prose poems, and brief lyric essays. There is even a companion crow with one foot, René, who, like the speaker, is compelling and brilliant and makes no promises. Deft with figurative language—'Like restaurant carp, we are learning to live in this aquarium,'—France de Bravo also questions the whole enterprise. 'Metaphors can seem so transactional, language doing business, swapping currency,' she writes, in a *zuihitsu* on giving and taking. Nothing here is undisputable, even the tools of the trade, and I love it. I love her parables breathing contemporary life into twelfth-century Tibetan Buddhist slogans on mind training—'And then, there was the time I drove a dangerous highway, / thumb-drive buried in my bun . . . files and poems bobby-pinned / to my skull.' I love the poems on flood and fire and plague, on dryer lint and home improvement, on the subject/object conundrum, on the woman, a mature, exhilarative presence, and on the one-legged crow, who has the first word, and the last."

—Diane Seuss, Pulitzer Prize–winning author
of *frank: sonnets* and *Modern Poetry*

"The muse of this collection is a one-legged crow, and crow it does, with an insinuating, insistent music and a wily, restless aesthetic that hops from brilliant image to sly aphorism to tender insight. These poems are luminously dark, keenly observant, and endlessly curious about the whole symphony of existence, where nothing is lost, everything is transformed, and we live our lives 'not dying, but molting.' *Locomotive Cathedral* is marked by its unflinching yet compassionate gaze; we are blessed to have it."

—Michael Bazzett, author of *The Echo Chamber*

"Brandel France de Bravo's *Locomotive Cathedral* is a panoramic meditation ushering us into stillness. With grace and humility, in a skillful range of forms, France de Bravo sings a praise song to surrender. When living means 'cycling through the stink and stain,' France de Bravo celebrates the sacred pause, reminding us that 'any raised surface can be an altar, a place to kneel.'"

—Rage Hezekiah, author of *Yearn*

The Backwaters Prize in Poetry Honorable Mention

for Mario and Amaya
　　my engines and sanctuary

Nothing is lost, nothing is created, everything is transformed.
    ANTOINE LAVOISIER, founder of modern chemistry

Contents

Regard the Other as a Verb 1

Part 1. Take & Give

After the Ecstasy, the Laundry 5
Resilience I 7
Free Trade Agreement, a *Zuihitsu* 8
Women Talking 10
Love It or List It 12
Staging 13
People of the Dog 14
Resilience II 15
Resilience III 16
You're Like a Dull Knife 17
The Lounge Chair Does the Work 18
Taking Dictation 19
Home Improvement 20
Pronominal Affection 21
It's a Joy to Be Hidden and a Disaster Not to Be Found 23
Fractals 24

Part 2. Mind Training Slogans

Slogan 27: Work with the Greatest Defilements First 31
Slogan 25: Don't Talk about Injured Limbs 32
Slogan 7: Giving and Taking Should Be Practiced Alternately.
These Two Should Ride the Breath (a.k.a. Practice *Tonglen*) 34
Slogan 34: Don't Transfer the Ox's Load to the Cow 36
Slogan 8: Three Objects, Three Poisons, Three Seeds of Virtue 37
Slogan 1: Train in the Preliminaries 40
Slogan 20: Of the Two Witnesses, Hold the Principal One 41

Slogan 38: Don't Seek Others' Pain as the Limbs
of Your Own Happiness 42
Slogan 49: Always Meditate on
Whatever Provokes Resentment 43
Slogan 59: Don't Expect Applause 44
Slogan 4: Self-Liberate Even the Antidote 48
Slogan 28: Abandon All Hope of Fruition 49

Part 3. After the Before Times

Resilience IV 53
What It Took and What It Gave 56
Resilience V 58
Lying Flat 59
Seam and Sieve 60
Tradition Is the Prison in Which You Live 61
Provincetown 62
Angrief 64
Now You Don't See It, Now You Do 65
If It's in the Way, It Is the Way 68
Resilience VI 69

Part 4. Terminal Lucidity

Resurrection, a Cento from My Murdered Darlings 73
As Seen on TV 75
Guns and Butter 76
The Chemistry of Distance 77
Course Correction 81
Gold Chains and Squash Blossoms 82
Wind in a Box 84
Final Descent 85
Resilience VII 86

Acknowledgments 87
Notes 91

Locomotive Cathedral

Regard the Other as a Verb

I don't eat crow. I feed crow.
My crow isn't *my* crow.
I name the crow because
I'm human and want to know
how a god feels. When I use my app
to ID a tree, I pronounce it
"Osage-orange." I bask
in my beneficence. I'm the Pope
tossing blessings from a balcony.
The crowd pecks at them,
gobbles them up. I am not
so different from a pigeon.
What appears to be strutting
is gracelessness on earth.

René is perspicacious
and has only one foot. Strutting
is out of the question. If I stare
at my balcony long enough,
he will glide toward it, flat
as a black manta ray. He is
my lesson in *looms large*.
Every visit is a spell. The sun
has a brief brown-out,
and I turn a little electric.

Maybe the crow and I are
planets. He likes orbs: grapes
and blueberries. Sometimes
his eating and my reading align.
And then, he leaves. A lesson

in *recede*. I watch until he bends
around a building. I have
a special whistle to call him,
but he is not a dog. The dachshund
next door barks for hours
when my neighbor goes out.
René caws on my railing
for what seems like hours. This
is my lesson in forgiveness.
He caws for me, for food,
for me with food. For me
to count 1-2-3 and throw
kibble for him to catch.

Every time I'm with him
I have to reprimand myself:
"Want, use your indoor voice!"

PART 1
Take & Give

After the Ecstasy, the Laundry

Window caulk cracking, door padlocked, another laundromat
is closing. How far will people have to drive their dirty
bedspreads? Headlights in daytime, snaking in slow caravans,

black Hefty bags in the back seat, to some suburban strip mall's
Sit and Spin. My years of hoarding quarters, jam-jar maracas
are over. Wheeling my wet load past oversized peepholes

as I eye the red minutes—over. I don't have a private
chapel devoted to laundry as seen on HGTV, just
an "in-unit W/D." And, so must most neighbors. Do I miss

laundromats? Maybe I miss the locker room–like looking,
the furtive interest surely shared given the rule
to never air. Maybe I miss balling socks, folding

underwear, quickly concealing the crotch, on a long table
where so many strangers' boxers, nightgowns have rested.
Any raised surface can be an altar, a place to kneel

side by side, mouths open to receive, eyes fixed ahead,
staring into a sleeve. Another laundromat is closing,
and I'm wistful for some imagined leveling, a there-but-

for-the-grace gone, forgetting there's always been drop-off
and laundresses like silent confessors to pound stone, wring
river, inhale the steam of hot metal communing with cotton.

From a stacked dryer in the closet, I carry my tangled
heap to the bed, spilling as I go. Is it lonely? Only
as much as meditation. Fishing and folding, I think:

justice like laundry is never over, which feels profound
until in a bookstore I discover I'm not the first
to find wisdom at the bottom of a hamper. Maybe it's

not how we do it but that we all do, cycling through
the stink and stain of it. An idea so soft from
billions of washings, you can't help wanting to wear it.

Resilience I

Like restaurant carp, we are learning to live in this aquarium. Whenever a whiff of mildew finds me, I imagine the taste of the cashier's mints—as good as bleach. Yesterday, I woke up peering through the slats of my bed and thought: *I sleep on a bridge.* The sea visits several times a year, like a family member from the mainland who stays too long. On the radio, they say it's rising, but who are we to stop it? I tie knots in the curtains, hang bags of rice I cannot cook on the clothesline, anchor every plastic chair with what must stay dry: the sewing machine I use to hem our skirts, pants—three times now—and cardboard boxes of family photos, foreign magazines, birth certificates, letters home, a diploma. The baby naps in her hammock, quiet catch, while my son pushes a flip-flop across the kitchen pond, making motor sounds with his mouth. In a few years, he will join his father and the other fishermen. The jerry cans of drinking water, half-full, are chained like floating dogs. I miss our rooster's *kikiriki*, but an ear acquires new habits: every liquid footstep bubbling inside me like oxygen.

Free Trade Agreement, a *Zuihitsu*

> *The* Tonglen *meditation practice of "taking and giving" is sometimes referred to as an exchange of self with other.*

I.

What is a handshake but a border crossing? Give and take, tit for tat, scratch my back. Your drugs for my guns. Trigger to temple, the ski mask asks: *¿plata o plomo?* "Silver or lead?" means money or a bullet to the head. *To be* (as in "alive") is a linking verb, while negotiation is excuse for relation. *You insult them if you pay asking.* Everyone loves a bargain, but don't strike one like it's a piñata.

II.

The Texas businessman says to the minister of transportation visiting from (   ), "See that highway? Ten percent of it right here," patting his breast pocket. Two years later, the Texan travels to his foreign friend's country. The minister says, "See that bridge over there?" "No," squints the Texan. "One hundred percent right here," the minister beams, patting the pocket of his (   ). Quid pro whoa, thinks the Texan, that's a bridge too far.

III.

A compromise spans two shores. Two lanes—one for coming, one for going—suspended over a body of water. Call the body "yielding," even as it churns. Somebody compromised is one who lives in suspense. When one partner peddles withholding, what is the balance of trade?

IV.

On a beach *so far from God and so close to the U.S.*, the Mexican masseur confides he saw Jesus "as close as that palm tree" and knows Coke's secret ingredient. In our jellied bliss, we don't dismiss him. If the red and white cans contain the blood of children, so does the green flesh on my toast, the *guac* on your chip. Blood diamonds, blood avocados—these are metaphors. Like pounding money over stones in a dirty river.

V.

Metaphors can seem so transactional, language doing business, swapping currency. But what if exchange is just a cover for change? *Nothing is lost, everything is transformed.* Then, give me a bucket brimming with blood to ferry across the river. I promise not to spill a drop, and when I reach the other side, I'll feed you what has turned viscous, golden, sweet.

VI.

Give and take, a marriage makes. Our bodies draw a heart in the middle of the bed: nose-to-nose, curved spines, a meeting of toes. But before long, I turn away to the cool edge where sleep awaits, where I don't have to inhale you. How many breaths have we traded? How much of me in you and you in me? We freely disagree. Call the body "yielding." Still, we churn.

Women Talking

Three friends in a hotel room, towel-wrapped
or pulling clothes from suitcases, each of us
narrating as we move through the morning.

"*Women Talking*!" I laugh, having just seen
the movie where Mennonite mothers, wives,
daughters gather to decide if they should stay

put and confront the men or leave and start
their own colony. No one has broken into
our suite, sprayed us with horse tranquilizer,

raped us in our sleep, which isn't to say
we've never been hurt. We're women:
talking to ourselves. *I think I'll shower*

when I come back. I should pack an umbrella
just in case. This panel looks really good,
one of us says while gazing at her phone,

the "this" invisible, a sedative hiss.
In our two-queen-bed colony, we don't need
to see to believe her. Like the writers

we are, we're reading our drafts aloud.
In grad school, we joked "it's a draft until
you die." That was over twenty-five years ago.

We're closer now. We're the kind of drivers
who signal our turns at 2:00 a,m., no one else
on the road. This noisy consideration

as we stare out the window at the parking lot
below, disposable coffee cups in hand,

emptying and refilling our backpacks,

brushing our hair next to paintings not meant
for looking at. When the click, click, click, doesn't
shut off as it should, I always have to tell

my husband, *your turn signal's still on*.
All the sounds only women seem to hear.

Love It or List It

Do you know the show's premise? A real
estate agent, interior designer, and a couple
with a checklist of needs who must choose
between a new house and their old remodeled.
Pull up stakes, or reframe the past and forego
a never-inhabited future? I've been trying

to let go of habits that linger like garage-sale
remains: the need to patch your roof, fix
your flashing. As though we could fool the rain.
Some rooms are unlovable. I could redecorate
(call this hunger "fasting") or move somewhere
with an open floor plan, no wall between

how I'm feeling and what you're seeing. *Every
criticism, judgment, diagnosis, expression
of anger is the tragic expression of an unmet
need.* Every time your face says "stop talking,"
and I want to leave. How do I decide if I don't
have a list of boxes to tick? One partner

on *Love It or List It* always asks for a giant
laundry room, where the systole and diastole
whoosh of the washer-dryer masks any sobs,
a gentle sac for the release of secretions where
I might float among the folded piles, warm and
soothing as a mother's voice muffled by viscera.

Staging

The countertop we'd always wanted, glistening with bits
of recycled glass, a new stove (built-in, not slide-out),
a barn door that conceals the washer-dryer stacked
in its alcove. We didn't painstakingly choose, design,
order, pay for, install any of these for *us* to enjoy.

When the house sold, we looked around, a mix of regret
and admiration, asked ourselves why we'd waited,
why we hadn't believed ourselves deserving of a home
like this: completed, perfectly staged with furniture
that belongs to no one. We'd begun the project

years ago, a gut remodel. It wore us down, drained
our savings. At some point, we must have decided,
although no one said it: "This is good enough."
Cancer came like a flyer slipped under the door,
invasive, raising questions. *Looking to sell your house?*

Are we? Should we? We circumambulate the young
clustered on the sidewalk outside the oyster bar,
clutching drinks, and my hand reaches for yours.
In the public park, we hold hands, wondering why
we'd waited as we stroll past the haunting purple

of an artichoke thistle in bloom, extraterrestrial.

People of the Dog

The taxi driver tells us Chichimeca means *perro amarado*: a tied-up dog. Chichimeca, the nomadic people who "overran," once ran this part of Mexico: lower than the tagless roamers of streets, than guards exiled to a roof that howl and howl. There's a joke I've heard many times since marrying into this country, culture. "The neighbor's dog barked all night long. I couldn't sleep." "Why were you listening?" goes the punchline, its wisdom irrefutable. But the taxi driver is confusing rope with lineage. Either way a cur is involved. Either way a slur. Chichimeca like Goth, Vandal, Hun. "Why are conquering barbarians always from the north?" asks the gringo, how I refer to myself—preemptive strike—among Mexicans. *Para el mexicano la vida es una posibilidad de chingar o de ser chingado*, wrote the Nobel poet. Fuck or be fucked. The Chichimecas were the OGs, *chingones*, until Spaniards, until gold, until tremorous smelting, vapor of mercury. Hordes vs. hoarders. I think you know the outcome. Did you know a murder scene smells of metal? Like the changing-room locker with a rusted padlock at the end of the school year, one blood goes unclaimed. Even though everyone's is supposed to be "mixed." The myth of mongreltude: Mexico's manifest destiny. In Spanish, handcuffs are called wives, and *tied-up* sounds a lot like *loved*. What if it's not about loosening the rope? What if loving the knot?

Resilience II

Feast on bitter milkweed, nourishment
and nursery. Store its poison like revenge
against the frog, bird, lizard, mouse
who would prey on your tiger stripes. And,
when the days grow shorter, join a caravan
bound for Mexico that inflames no one.
Something there is that doesn't love
a wall. Leave Canuck-cold, bootstraps, self-
made, go-it-alone. Be unexceptional as you fly
en masse, no air traffic control, three thousand
miles to a gentler fall, Day of the Dead,
marigolds, coxcomb, and candles, your one
and only visit to Mexico a heralded return:
all hail the monarchs. Huddle in oyamel furs

on steep slopes at night, breaking branches
with your featherweight, and once the sun
has finally warmed you, give the royal wave
of a million orange gloves. You'll bear heirs
in spring, pass the crown, but until then,
live from your larder in diapause. *Our* feast,
bitter as milkweed, never slows, and heat's

the poison we store. It's causing oyamel to die,
at least the ones not logged. How do you rescue
a winter palace in ruins? Plant the forest higher
where it's cooler, say the scientists, like a house
on stilts. Deferred Action for Climate Ailments?
Dreamers, we hunt and hunt for higher ground,
seeding uphill. Where fire travels fastest.

Resilience III

Fire is an aria, not a red curtain.
What survived? A filing cabinet,
a pair of diamond earrings, a skillet.

Fire is a sermon, not a pulpit.
What survived? A wedding ring
of gold, a hacksaw, a wrench.

Fire is push and tear, not an infant.
What survives? The blue taste
of colostrum, defense against.

Fire is a contest, not a medal.
What survived? A porcelain sink,
two spoons, a knife, some bricks.

What's born in fire will not burn.
What survives? The memory of being
undone, re-formed: to *forge* ahead.

Fire is a gasp for breath, not a corpse.
What survived? Seeds of scrub pine,
lodge pole and jack, sleeping beauties

all waiting for a furnace kiss.

You're Like a Dull Knife

> *In 2000 James Brown lost forty years of memorabilia, including unreleased songs and a preacher's cape in a fire.*

It's the dull knife you have to watch out for, my mother used to say. It's 6:00 a.m.—too early for frying—and the hallways smell of fish. The man from the apartment next door is patrolling, eyeing the one flickering light, hand held to wall, sniffing. *It might be an electrical fire.* The building is silent, ours the only alarm. What if all our insulation went up in smoke? Maybe it's a houseguest who stayed more than three days, trapped like a hamster behind drywall. This happened with ours. Twice. We were remodeling, baseboards not yet installed. More than death and its unlocatable rot, we worried about chewed wires, smolder of plastic, invisible burn. We lured out the all-black hamster—Charcoal—with bacon, a scent I, too, would gladly follow into a locked cage. Trying to write inside a building that might be burning is a parable. Because the dull knife doesn't seem to cut, you put your weight into it. Words. *Talkin' Loud and Sayin' Nothing.*

The Lounge Chair Does the Work

All the chairs committed to doing the work. *It's time each of us interrogates our role in this household.* But no one had any questions. Only statements released like shiny foil balloons that rise in the air and tremble against the ceiling.

"As someone who is bi-positional . . ." started the recliner.

"As a squishy sack full of beans, I can speak to the experience of low."

"As a seat living with prolapse, I want to acknowledge the hurt and discomfort I've caused actual butterflies."

"As a straight-back, I reject the label 'dining.' I am so much more than a room."

"As a gilt and velvet-covered—" All the chairs shot the throne a look, and the wheelchair left the room sighing, "I am just so exhausted." This prompted the chairs to murmur "self-care" to one another approvingly.

The statements resumed. No one was too inquisitive. Each chair was certain it knew the other's angle of repose. Who was accommodating, whose springs were broken. When all the chairs had finished sharing, the rocker suggested a game: "Alexa, play some music!" All the chairs began shuffling behind one another in a circle. When the music stopped, every chair was in a different place from the start, and no one was "out."

Taking Dictation

I'm Berlusconi minus the pomade, Putin's twenty bottles
of vodka and birthday mash note. *You're one of my five
real friends.* Just as a poet always writes for other poets,
an authoritarian is only authentic with his own kind.
"Expropriate that!" I shout like Chavez as I walk the streets
checking for my portrait in every government office.

I'm Bokassa sans crocodiles, a Mobutu who lacks branding:
*The all-powerful warrior who, because of his endurance
and inflexible will to win, goes from conquest to conquest,*

leaving fire in his wake. Last night, I dreamed I woke up
to tiny dusty footprints marching across my bedroom floor:
hard-soled shoes with pointy toes. Auguring? I'm not sure.

I'm Ceaușescu without the scepter or bronze yak from Mao,
running a police state the size of Candyland. Being feared
is often confused with being loved. If only I could dictate *that*.

Make me magnetic, something you can't help wanting
to grab from an oversized suit pocket. Strip me of my envelope
for all to read. Pull comes with push, you say? I'll take that.

I'm Kim Jong Un's letter—nothing but memories on my back.
Even in exile, I'm a star. I can do anything. Watch me burn down
this gulag they call archives. Hot blue, red giant, white dwarf.

Home Improvement

> How much larger your life would be
> if your self could be smaller in it.
> —G. K. Chesterton

You could demolish a few rooms or annex the empty lot, an acre
to enlarge your plot. Remodeling is a bitch. Ask any architect: better
to build from scratch. Try translucent cement, the latest in facades.
Waterproof, it can withstand quakes—as if it were an "I" that refused
rigidity. Construct the house, then take it apart. Arrange the materials
on the ground: bricks, beams, nails, planks, windows, a door. In pieces,
is it still your home? Mostly, the "I" feels like an eye, or a conductor.
But what if you peer into the pit and there's no orchestra? It's science
when we say the act of looking affects what's looked at. We take
the corollary on faith: *when we are observing love, we are that love.*
Do you see a woman in a black sheath, chin pinned to violin, or some
wireless speakers? Your mind isn't separate; it isn't even yours. Like
the patch of grass between the sidewalk and street that you water
and weed. It doesn't belong to you, and no one else picks up the litter.

Pronominal Affection

New Caledonian crows have the intelligence
                                    of seven-year-olds.
Where's the "I" in your poems? I can't always tell
who's speaking   or to whom?
A kid who's seven can make Halloween candy
                        last until Thanksgiving,
        and a crow will turn down a second-rate treat
for a tool that unlocks   a better reward later on.
I'm talking to you, or maybe my crow,
                or someone I love, assuming
they love me,   which I shouldn't.
Caledonian crows can join two tubes,
                fit one inside the other
to create a key   that opens a puzzle box.
How deep is your lock?
                You is a compound tool.
                            It has great reach.
Stay awhile so I can admire the blue
                of you in the morning sun,
        your third eyelid sweeping
from inner   to outer corner.

Give me that profile

        one more time.   Wait.

            Let me get my phone to capture
you.

      What are you thinking? What does this

         relationship involve, really?

Is it just about me   feeding you

      words?

Do you like me in glasses? With my hair up?

     I know you can see through

my presentation, whatever   it is today.

Crows never forget   a face.

    Finally, he eats

      from my hand. I don't know if that's trust

           or confidence in escape.

     The ease with which you can look away.

When I call you *a good boy*, do you feel closer to me?

    I'm willing to say, here on this balcony,

          to you on that railing,

    what I've never said   to anyone before.

That is the point of this, right?

It's a Joy to Be Hidden and a Disaster Not to Be Found

Pink Floyd the flamingo, Inky the octopus, the Roomba
that ran away from the Travelodge in Cambridge.
I collect escape artists like quotes, bizarre headlines.
"House Hunting on Mars Has Already Started," reads
the paper of record. Wheeling my shopping cart past
tabloids, I come to the bouquets and an empty bucket
labeled "filler flowers." What does it mean to be seen?

Yesterday, I saw a homeless man, high and jackknifed
over a trash can, the bloom of him buried. Another driver
stopped, got out of his car, and then my light turned green.
How fast, how far can I move from what discomfits me?
You could say I'm learning object permanence, still playing
peek-a-boo. Whether it's a windshield or words, I'm always
trying to hide behind glass. I want to be the wallflower

watching *me* be the life of the party. No wonder writing
feels like a dark theater where I toggle between the screen
and the exit sign's glow. My fears aren't original or deep:
unable to quickly surface is reason enough to never scuba dive.
Tunnels: there's a light at the end, they say, but that sounds
a lot like a bottomless bucket to me. Every runaway wants
to be caught, brought home. Otherwise, it's just travel.

Fractals

Alec and his American father meet in a hotel room. Two years have passed since the war ended, and more than that since father and son last saw each other. British accent fading, Alec is finally fitting in at Shaker Heights High. The father is staying at the Cleveland Hotel in the Terminal Tower Building.

When does a sequence of events become a story? How much transformation must occur, how much distillation? Bullet, bottle, barbiturate.

Evacuated during the Blitz and sent to Ohio to live with his paternal grandparents, Alec loves American football. He also loves his British mother who speaks German, stayed in England to crack the code, and will never again live with her son. His father, a U.S. diplomat—Vienna, Cairo, Mexico City—decided to enlist. Alec's parents give up on the marriage, divorce.

In the hotel room, the diplomat invites Alec to live with him in Washington, D.C. Alec wonders why his father is staying in a hotel and not the Shaker Heights house where he grew up and where Alec is now growing up. The diplomat tells his son he's brought him a present from Japan. "Open the drawer." Alec picks the wrong dresser drawer. Many bottles clink brown and gold against each other. The diplomat closes the drawer and from another pulls out a pair of binoculars, which he gives his son.

I use these binoculars every day, standing on my balcony, scanning the sky, waiting for my crow to come.

Alec was my stepfather.

*

The next day, in a room at the Cleveland Hotel, in the Terminal Tower building, the diplomat shoots himself. One of the drawers Alec didn't open.

Alec adopted me after marrying my mother. His name appears next to "father" on my amended birth certificate. He was as good to me as I allowed. Bill, the blood father I mostly knew through legend, was rock to his paper. Absence like scissors.

Bill: serial fatherer, beatnik poet, drunken brawler, gun and weed runner, botcher of plans, including to assassinate Franco, felon, writer of prison letters.

How does repetition become a fugue?

Alec never told me to open his medicine cabinet or top dresser drawer, the one he used to keep his hash in. As a teenager, I shaved off bits thinking he'd never notice. If, on one of my visits home from graduate school, he had told me to look inside, I might have found a prescription bottle for the powerful and now-discontinued sedative Tuinal. I wouldn't have asked him why. I'd have pocketed one.

Sifting through his papers—short stories, letters never sent, poems—after he died, I found this: "The things that I must do are my undoing."

Every story needs a conflict and a resolution. If conflict is a knot, is resolution the undoing?

**

Bill, my biological father, came calling six months before his last bender. The one doctors assured him would end his life, and did at thirty-nine. Bill wanted to know his daughter, a daughter, *this* daughter. Yellow-eyed but sober, he knocked at the apartment door. I was alone; my mother and Alec would come home two hours later and find us together. Seated at our round dining room table, Bill said, "Let's call Pops and Gypsy." I was thirteen and understood these to be my grandparents. He told me to reach into his coat pocket. I pulled out a bag of weed. "No, the other pocket." In it, a small address book.

Would this be a better story had it been a glassine envelope of heroin in his pocket, an overdose six months later?

Because he died young, Bill became a lake no wind could touch, water on which my imagination could float undisturbed in sunglasses, cup holder overflowing.

***

At the time of his suicide, Alec was a few years older than his father had been. Neither my mother nor I was living with him. They had given up on the marriage, separated. Alec was sixteen when his father shot himself. I was twenty-six when Alec's letter arrived with a check: "Deposit this *toute suite*, the touter, the sweeter." The handwriting collapsing, slumped over. By that time, Bill had already been dead twelve years.

It's never about chronology, is it?

In college, I thought about becoming a diplomat, but I failed the foreign service exam. In my early twenties, I left Washington, D.C., where I'd been born and raised, for Cairo, New York, Mexico City, other elsewheres. In my thirties, I married and got an MFA. Drugs and alcohol eventually grew small, like looking through the wrong end of binoculars.

It's about what you include. What do you choose to omit?

What I'm leaving out: one of Bill's grandchildren. Bullet, high school parking lot. But this story isn't mine to tell.

****

After Alec had had one too many affairs, my mother left him. He started playing solitaire with old photos on the round dining room table, the blinds drawn. Of the many diagnoses he was given, depression was not among them. What he never said to me: "Would you consider coming back here to live?"

There is a science of regret. The pain from what we said or did is never as great as the pain from what we didn't.

Why would I have responded any differently from a gangly high school boy who wanted to stay in Shaker Heights, play football, finally fit in?

What is the right tense for this?

Alec injures his back playing football in college. Many surgeries later and wearing a brace, he graduates, takes the Foreign Service exam, and passes. The back pain comes and goes; sick days are used up. He realizes he'll never be posted overseas, never leave Washington, D.C., the place he'd refused as a boy. He gives up on being a diplomat, becomes an English literature professor.

Fractals: in which similar patterns recur at progressively smaller scales, from the Latin fract—*"broken," from the verb* frangere.

*****

I'm writing this in my apartment in Washington, D.C., a city I never thought I'd return to. Orphan, mother, wife, writer, I am content with my discontentment. Broken, alive.

Before a one-footed crow started visiting my balcony, I rarely noticed birds. I'm thinking of buying a new pair of binoculars—without scratched lenses, lighter around my neck.

PART 2
Mind Training Slogans

Tibetan Buddhist teachings on mind training, known as *lojong*, were condensed and arranged into fifty-nine sayings or slogans in the twelfth century. The slogans are tools for reducing self-grasping and cultivating compassion.

Slogan 27
WORK WITH THE GREATEST DEFILEMENTS FIRST

I can hold a grudge against water. Life's always been scarce for me.
The way it runs down a forearm, off the elbow to pool on the floor

as I wash my face, the uncontrollable waste. The way failure
clings like two wet sleeves. When I wing it and flop, there's guilt

(blame it on my lack of discipline). When I rehearse and miss,
I feel shame for all God hasn't given me. There are rituals

for stanching loss, distributing risk, and who doesn't resent
involuntary donation? Blood, years, belongings. A parking ticket

left on the windshield protects, but one bite from a mosquito,
one cancer, can't defend you against another. Phone, cash, cards

must be stashed in different undergarments, pockets whenever I leave
the house. And then there was the time I drove a dangerous highway,

thumb drive buried in my bun. I stood beside the empty road, lined
with shade-less mesquites, watching the carjackers speed away,

my suitcase and computer in the trunk, files and poems bobby-pinned
to my skull. All those years, I thought it was profligacy, the eleven

children my father once boasted of having by almost as many women.
This was a dinner party in the seventies, population a ticking bomb.

What will you do when we run out of space? a disgusted guest asked.
My father stood up and slurred, *I'll make room,* flinging his arms wide.

Not even my passwords are retrievable without a password.

Slogan 25
DON'T TALK ABOUT INJURED LIMBS

They look like kangaroos at the beach
—older white people, doubled over
the edge of Florida's Gulf, wearing
belly bags. They're eyeing the sand
for sharks' teeth, black and abundant
on this stretch of coast. With their visors
and sun-slapped skin, slick with lotion,
are *these* my people? Others walk upright
with what appear to be golf clubs, a sieve
to sift tooth from chaff at the base.
Every ten feet, another dead fish,
even an iguana in Savasana.
The humans greet each other and cough.
"Red tide tickle," they call it.
Some sneeze or wheeze. No one's
swimming. Just collecting, collecting.

One woman tells me, "I can't stop
even when I have a Ziploc bag full.
It's so relaxing." She reaches in
and hands me a fistful of teeth.
I thank her and think of Carlos's sister,
who he says can't unwind, only finds
peace shopping all night online
and sleeps by day. I'm judging again.
I can't stop. I observe, then categorize
just as I do the shells underfoot:
"ice cream cone," "pock-marked,"
"Ruffles potato chip." I walk some more
before recalling something I heard

in a podcast: *joyful participation
in a world of sorrows*. Why assume
the beachcombers are choosing
to ignore warming waters, algal bloom?
Are averting their gaze from the ways
some joys lead to others' sorrow?

A woman with binoculars who prefers
categories of birds to shells, up to down,
watches bald eagles dive and grasp
what floats on the Gulf's surface.
"I didn't know eagles could be seabirds,"
I tell her. "They'll eat carrion wherever
they find it," she says, and for a minute
I reconsider our national symbol
—taloned, carcass-loving—on the back
of every dollar bill. For centuries
Parsis left their dead at the Tower
of Silence, not wanting to taint water
or land. I'm grateful bald eagles
haven't disappeared like the vultures
of Mumbai. "Sky burial," they called it.

My walk almost done, I notice no one
empties their stash before leaving
the beach. The collection plate in this
church is replete, after all. The teeth
shift and click against coins, keys,
pens in the pocket of my backpack.
The teeth are hard and sharp like more.

Slogan 7
GIVING AND TAKING SHOULD BE PRACTICED ALTERNATELY.
THESE TWO SHOULD RIDE THE BREATH (A.K.A. PRACTICE *TONGLEN*)

for Ahmaud Arbery

Could I carve into another's calf as if a bruised pear
        Didn't I light a bowl, suck the pipe, fill my throat

and place my lips there to suck, draw out the venom,
        and lungs with smoke, then gesture with my eyes

spit on the ground before looking up at pained eyes,
        for a friend to come close so I could blow a blend

without worry about what lingers or is crawling
        of weed and me into her open mouth? Shotgun!

even now toward the heart? I'm not some TV cowboy,
        You could receive, give, or if you called it first,

but I'll ride shotgun, the "death-seat." Where else to sit?
        ride up front, next to the one at the steering wheel.

The world is a shotgun shack, one room piercing the next.
        I inhale suffering, blue as the smoke from her cigarette.

Your frack, my tap. My fire, your smoke. Her cough.
> *One blue cloud spills into the next. A few wisps. She died*

Some of my cells still inside her, like old love letters.
> *from cells that divide and conquer. And the father who quit*

And the man who filled the vacancy and killed himself, too,
> *the job, then walked out on life—I grew lilacs in his fallow.*

but let me eat and eat and eat without ever saying grace
> *And the grown child I couldn't protect: I breathe in breach,*

while I waited for hunger's return. Sometimes, the stranger
> *cradling us both in the palm of my outbreath. Shotgun*

is strangely dear. I inhale pursuit and exhale wind at the jogger's
> *used to mean the passenger who had the wagon driver's back,*

back, lifting him into the air, over the white pickup, the armed
> *an armed lookout. Between a snake bite and the heart—map it.*

white men and half-built houses, high above the gated desolation.
> *Ocean waters rising, closing off the road like a tourniquet.*

Slogan 34
DON'T TRANSFER THE OX'S LOAD TO THE COW

I've measured out my life in dryer lint. Do I dare,
with my father's eyes, follow a swallow in the air?

All that I can't hold. The stutter, dip, and glide of it.
All the scraping, clumping, dutiful disposing of it.

Everything transpired, gone, lives on like a mother.
Handing a morning mug to my daughter, she hovers.

Who is the hanger and who is the dress? I digress.

What I mean to say is I've never once seen my head
from behind. Maybe it's a billboard where you read

my uncharitable thoughts about you, them, myself,
pinned and wriggling on the wall. I'd love to be a MILF,

but who feels sexy with a tumorous growth? The bloat.
No way to know whether I'm someone's guest or host.

It reminds me of that fable. When the dolorous donkey
carries both old man and boy, they say, "Animal cruelty."

"Call Child Protection" should the man decide to ride
while the kid walks, whining, by the donkey's side.

"Selfish youth" when it's reversed, the old man
shuffling in the dirt. "Stupidity" if neither human

on the journey mounts the beast. Millenia-old
moral: try to please all and you'll please none.

No matter my footwork, how I dodge and feint,
shame's punch always lands. It's the heavyweight.

The load I take off your back and put onto mine.

Slogan 8
THREE OBJECTS, THREE POISONS, THREE SEEDS OF VIRTUE

Object

You are my subject. The you I gave my locker combination to, the confidant under my comforter, the you I would break quarantine for. (Here the "you" begs for more, to become an exclusive "we.")

The you I would abandon a full shopping cart to avoid, the you I put a hex on—make her sell, move away!—almost turning our party wall into a wake. (Second-person can be a ball thrown at instead of to.)

The you whose email fell from a window, and I never looked down. The you I introduce myself to at every party, promising *this* time I'll remember her name. (Here, "you" is closer to third person, almost "it.")

Friend, enemy, stranger—object to the label. Legible and smooth on one side, sticky on the other. Peel it off, examine what clings. Pleasant, unpleasant, meh. You think: make it stay, make it go away, make it nothing. For each object, a verb: desire, despise, disconnect.

Poison

In a dive bar in the Amazon, the Buddhist points to a dartboard between the jukebox and bathroom to explain: "Three poisonous darts pin us to the wheel. Greed, aversion, and delusion." Taking a sip of beer, the toxicologist wonders who *us* is. "In my country," the Buddhist continues, "we have no bull's-eye. At the center of the wheel are a rooster, a snake, and a pig. For each poison, an animal." The toxicologist's face lights up with the chance to impart *his* wisdom: "The dose makes the poison!" He knows there is medicine in the glands of tropical toads; his robed drinking partner who doesn't drink knows there is cure in human muck. Eat any part of the yew at your peril, but in its bark is a chemical that will kill the cancer killing you. Last year, pit viper venom saved more hearts than it stopped. What, you ask, are *my* poisons? If I interrupt incessantly, replacing your words with mine, it must be because I crave braiding myself with another until we are thick as rope. Or is it just I hate waiting? Delusion's animal is the pig that roots, eyes buried in dirt. I have a drawer-full, given by well-meaning friends who'd heard I liked pigs: metal, coin-slotted, wooden, pepper-shaking, ceramic.

Virtue

Pull apart object and reaction. Separate them as you would two kids in a schoolyard scuffle. Seat them in an empty classroom facing one another, six feet apart. Let what transpired be a mobile suspended above them, twisting this way and that. No demerits, no detention. Only an expanse of linoleum between them to be turned over, aerated, sown. Senses, feelings bud and drop their petals in the brain. They no more belong to an object than yellow to the dandelion. *To our senses, things offer only their rejections.* What the gardenia wants: freedom from its perfume. Inhale it, unburden every flower.

Slogan 1
TRAIN IN THE PRELIMINARIES

The empty suitcase weighs too much to lift. Heavy in French, *lourde*, which makes me think holy, as in the waters. Before buying, I open it up, unbuckle the flaps, unzip every compartment, trying to figure out whether the hidden heft is dense—a few buried organs—or distributed like bacteria over the body. We roll home. The suitcase will hold everything I need and nothing to make my trip easier, the motel room less dank. The first item I pack is a black sachet, which I untie to check the contents after shifting years: a daughter's first breath, translucent inside velvet. Next to it, I tuck a bamboo box with my mother's ashes because I don't know what else to do with them. Nowhere good enough. I pack an almost empty bottle of cologne (*L'Air du Temps*), and toss in a razor, box of laundry detergent, and a book of verbs. Then, a boom box, a mix of '60s hits on a cassette tape (small wheels keep on turning), and a fine-toothed comb. I place a folded sweatshirt on top that reads, *This Isn't About Me* to pad the delicates. Wherever I spend the night, I'll comb my hair in the bathroom mirror, lip-synching, "Is that all there is to a fire?" With those fine teeth, I won't make it past the knotty ends, but I'll tease out any nits nested in my roots.

Slogan 20
OF THE TWO WITNESSES, HOLD THE PRINCIPAL ONE

Everything I've ever walked away from. The Greek diner with too many sides for my hungover mind that I left mid-shift, as in, "You can take off your apron and go." The work-study job that paid me to produce a paper I stayed on campus all summer after graduation not to write. The fiancé I flew to Geneva to tell in person, "We're through," emphasizing the seventeen-year difference in age, downplaying the man I'd met and did marry. Beneath my sense of duty, a floozie lighting one cigarette with another as she adjusts her slip. Everything I've walked away from. The guilt, or is it shame? The difference between lying and liar. The relief, or is it resurrection? The difference between finding your car in the underground parking and driving it through a desert on an empty highway. Obliging dinner guest, I left nothing on my plate, and *opa!* smashed it. When Hodja, Turkey's Aesop, returns a borrowed pot with a smaller pot nestled inside, he explains to his surprised neighbor, "It would not be right to separate the child from its mother." The next time the neighbor lends Hodja a pot, he waits and waits for its return. "If a cauldron can give birth, it can also die," snaps Hodja.

I should walk away more.

Slogan 38
DON'T SEEK OTHERS' PAIN AS THE LIMBS
OF YOUR OWN HAPPINESS

Schadenfreude is my housecoat, a little frock
I throw on for modesty's sake, your safety
because let's face it: I'm a knockout, got gams
like a Venn diagram, a fist like a fetal position.
My pleasure peeks from three-quarter sleeves
as I reach for a tray of bite-sized sausages.
Just look at my backstroke! I'm a waterwheel
catching your fall, grinding you into bread.
My corpuscles are pink slips, my liver all
you cannot forgive in yourself. Give me
your stooped, your sorry. Give me a head
hanging and I'll make a step stool. Take
a low blow and give me my pneumatic lift.

Slogan 49
ALWAYS MEDITATE ON WHATEVER PROVOKES RESENTMENT

in memory of Tom Lux

Writing in all lower case. *Relaxed but sitting tall.*
What a rebel! No, I get it: you're just humble.

The gratitude geyser. *Adopt a strong back, soft belly.*
A dozen Krispy Kremes a day and still skinny.

Changing lanes constantly. *Hands resting in the lap.*
A chihuahua underfoot: oversized balls and yapping.

Wet towel draped over the tub to "dry." *Take a deep breath.*
Two ways to kill a plant, and overwatering's your method.

Deciding not to have kids. *Eyes may be open or lightly closed.*
Time's scarce, too, hoarder. You have a low pain threshold.

The people of the other village. *Noticing the sounds around you.*
Wrong: an anagram of grown. As a prank, we mix their flour

at night with broken glass. Ask me if I miss the bread.

Slogan 59
DON'T EXPECT APPLAUSE

> Don't count on receiving credit for your good deeds.
> Just do them anyway!
> —Pema Chodron,
> commentary on Slogan 59, *The Compassion Book*

Circumstances aren't deeds.

I'm white and my father left my mother when she was pregnant with me. She raised me by herself until she married my stepfather when I was eight. While she worked, Howard University students babysat me. Two were named Maggie. One Maggie let me watch *Dark Shadows* with her when I came home from first grade. I learned that vampires live among us.

The stories I tell aren't deeds.

I'm white and attended Head Start. My mother asked what we did on our first day in the new program. "We sang the alphabet song and learned how to scrub the floor." This pleased my receptionist / cocktail waitress / secretary mother, who gave me a bucket of soapy water and a brush and left me in the kitchen. When she came back an hour and many cigarettes later, she found one sparkling linoleum tile among the dozens and one child engrossed in a picture book.

I'm white and I was on the swim team of my public pool, which closed on Labor Day. We didn't swim year-round, so we weren't "real" swimmers. None of the kids we competed against were. The difference was our team was almost all white. Sometimes when we swam at a rival team's pool, the kids watching on the other side of the fence would throw rocks at us on the starting block.

Multiple yeses on a test for Adverse Childhood Experiences aren't deeds.

I'm white and my father went to prison twice: Carabanchel in Madrid, where my mother's lawyer sent the divorce decree, and Leavenworth in Kansas.

I'm white and my mother caught me standing at the windowsill eating lead paint chips. Same city, decades later, my four-year-old daughter drank water every day from the tap—a public good—high in lead.

My confessions aren't deeds.

I'm white and had a safety net: grandparents with money. They disapproved of and cut my mother off, but a grandchild and a divorce lawyer were expenses they could justify.

People of color can't be considered confessional writers, says the poet Shane McCrae, even if they write autobiographically. "The confessional is the admitting of a step—or a fall—away from a state of grace.... The assumption behind it is that grace is a default position."

I'm white and I expect to be seen as one-of-a-kind, a sparkling individual. I can't remember if the Head Start teachers had given each of us one unlaid tile to practice on or assigned a section of the floor.

My feelings aren't deeds.

I'm white and went to Stevens Elementary School (named for Thaddeus Stevens, a "Radical Republican" abolitionist congressman from Pennsylvania). The only white girl in my class, I complained to my mother that the other kids wouldn't play with me. Later, when I made friends and came home saying "ain't," my mother slapped me.

My choices aren't deeds. Many of them aren't even choices.

I'm white and when Elektra, another white girl, blonde like me, showed up in second grade, told me "my momma learned me to read," I steered clear at recess.

I'm white and everyone in my mother's family went to college.

My will to impress isn't a deed.

I'm white and I've brought sandwiches, a blanket, and a sweatshirt with no cords to my Mexican husband in a Mexican jail.

I'm white and American, so I was outraged that he didn't get a phone call.

I'm white and I swam one summer with a Black swim team. I wasn't good enough to swim with them, but Vicky, the Black woman who coached at my public pool, invited some of us to swim with the famous Black team that she had belonged to when she was younger. I remember a swim meet at an all-white country club in the suburbs, white parents who didn't think Black people could swim sipping iced tea, and a pride that didn't belong to me when we won.

Proximity isn't a deed.

I'm white and my high school boyfriend's family didn't like me for that reason. Whenever I called him, one of his sisters would pick up the phone and shout, "David, it's the little white girl!" His family had two cars, but he was only allowed to take me in the old station wagon. His family didn't want me leaving my "long white hairs" on the new car's upholstery.

I'm white and thought I left no trace, could do no real harm. If my tenth grade history book mentioned the Scottsboro Boys, Emmitt Till, or any white woman's false accusation, I said I was a strand, not to be confused with a heavy head of hair.

My writing this isn't a deed.

I feel you reading this. As you look up, I can't help but search your face for a sign.

It's better if I look away, know that your hands are sleeping in separate beds and that what I hear is attentive silence: as if giving a concert in an opera house, a potted plant in every seat.

Slogan 4
SELF-LIBERATE EVEN THE ANTIDOTE

Fill the pool knowing full well it's not the end
of empty, that those who drained it—better no one
swim than together—planted oaks where water
was, a rustling shelter for fear. Cut them down,
knowing roots, acorns. Break ground, work around
clotted concrete, listen to the sound of shovel
against gravel. What does bone-weary even mean?
Be the cartilage that was never meant to last.

Slogan 28
ABANDON ALL HOPE OF FRUITION

Abandon the pith, the pit, and the peel
to its blackening. Abandon slogans
tobogganing toward salvation.
Abandon the imperative, and banal
numbered proclamations (*bannum* in Latin).
Abandon roots, pull them up at will:
as in *á bandon*. Abandon the red thread
you unwound from your pocket. Abandon
finding a way out and losing yourself.
Abandon "of"—so possessive, needy!
Abandon all for one and principle
for principal. Abandon LOIs, RFPs,
SOWs, SWOTs. Abandon fast and braking.
Abandon crossing more than the one
finish line. Abandon abandonment:
the story the apple keeps telling itself.
Abandon hope of someone pulling spine
from shelf, cracking to read. Abandon
through lines, concision, the perfect ending.
Abandon your distrust of morticians,
antimacassars, parlors. Abandon all to dirt,
dust, ashes, and to, to, to, too. Abandon
cottonwood and maple to the wind
and yew berries to badger bellies.

PART 3
After the Before Times

Resilience IV

> Attention, taken to its highest degree,
> is the same thing as prayer.
> —Simone Weil

Where you see COVID, I read corvid ever since a one-footed crow, imposing, totemic and gleaming black, came into my life, my only reliable companion in the pandemic. If a collection of crows is a murder, mine appears innocent. Is it true that crows hold funerals? What's clear is they feel absence. We have that in common.

*

When quarantine began, I bought a bird feeder for my balcony and a mix of seed for "urban birds" (code for I don't know what). Its smattering of peanuts lured a blue jay and my one-footed friend, but I was soon swamped by sparrows. They clustered, in defiance of the new norms, wing-to-wing inside the dish—toddlers in a ball pit at a fast-food restaurant—spilling food, covering my balcony, and the one below, with shit. I dispensed with seed in favor of crow delicacies—blueberries, dog kibble—too big for the chirping clouds of brown.

*

Unsure whether my solo crow wasn't perhaps a raven and of gender, I named them René(e). I studied their comings and goings, which balconies and roofs they perched on, the trees they flew to at dusk, and their caws and open-beak silences as they stared at me through the window. Little by little, they trusted me enough to visit while I sat on the balcony, watching. I admired how they balanced on the slippery steel railing and hopped on their one foot to the feeder, using their stump like a kickstand. I admired the strength in that one foot as it grasped the dish's rim, talons wrapped tight, allowing the bird to dip its beak into the dish and lose sight for a second of the potential predator, book-in-lap. I wondered how a bird as smart as a corvid, known for dropping nuts in the shell from telephone wires and swooping down to eat the meat after a car has driven over them, could have lost a foot. Who hasn't been the victim of poor timing—the overwhelming impulse to gossip about someone just as they're entering the room? It will be days, maybe weeks before I know if the needs or desires I fulfilled today put me in harm's way.

*

How much can a crow carry? Thief, trickster, minstrel Jim. One day, René(e) seized the plastic dish of kibble in their beak and flew away with it to my neighbor's less precarious terrace. All of us are turning to takeout, all of us seeking safety. Three black stones weigh down the new dish.

*

I'm not fooling myself. Loss of fear isn't attachment, and greedily taking what I give is not affection. Still, when this consumer of carrion lands next to me to drink, a few drops splashing my leg, I'm thrilled by contact with the water from their beak: foreign, intimate, and cool in the ninety-degree heat. Walking in my neighborhood to buy food, go to the hardware store, I sense I'm under surveillance. The crows are too high up to see if any are missing a foot, but I hear them like a new station on my radio dial where before there had been silence, static.

*

After a month or so, a two-footed crow, smaller than René(e), less ruffled, started showing up. Its sleeker build allowed a clear view of its legs and feet, strangely artificial in their perfection. René(e) and the new crow rarely come together, preferring to stagger their visits, one watching from a few stories above as the other eats and drinks. I assume that they are partners, which has forced me to reappraise René much as I reappraise daily this forced solitude, these many months separated from my husband by a border. COVID caught him like a thunderstorm, and he shelters in Mexico keeping his mother safe while worrying about his other family.

*

Now, I have two crows, like Rumi's two hands:

*If it were always a fist or always stretched open,
you would be paralyzed.*

*Your deepest presence is in every small contracting
and expanding,
the two as beautifully balanced and coordinated
as bird wings.*

*

Daily, my crows crisscross the alley sky, rapid shadows in the corner of my eye. I see their flight reflected in my glass coffee table, like Odin's two ravens, "thought" and "mind." The Norse god with only one eye relied on Huginn and Muninn as spies and advisors. My crows will never sit on my shoulders or whisper in my ear. They've never even brought me a shiny trinket, although René once left a cookie on my railing, which I took to be a gift until it disappeared. Still, I worry when I don't see René, just as I worry when I share the elevator with a neighbor who, like me, is hungry for exchange, for a peek behind the mask.

*

Starvation, predation—only half of crows survive their first year of life—the temptation of a run-over rat, a bite from a West Nile–infected mosquito: every danger surmounted is another twig in the nest. Without risk there can be no resilience, but survival, like love, demands our close attention. What looks to us like crows sitting *shiva* may be forensics in formation: *learn from this or get eliminated.* What happened? they seem to ask as they gather around the body.

What It Took and What It Gave

It took pants with zippers, hard-
soled shoes and Spanx.

It took tables in rows
reaching for bread baskets.

It took burnt coffee, unclaimed
sandwiches in office fridges.

It took jostling and dinner parties.

It took smells: cumin, hyacinth,
socks worn too many days.

It took the phone ring's sting
and invasion from the voice.

It took classrooms and the carrel's
simulacrum of solitude.

It took road rage, parking fines.

It took the frisson of the still-warm
bike seat at the gym.

It took cooing over strollers,
bending to pat a panting pug.

It took the worry a conjugal cough
would keep you from your sleep.

It took out-of-town guests.

It took canvases with captions
and curated murmurs.

It took buildings' bonnets,
skullcaps, and knees.

It gave travel-by-boat time,
ocean-liner mind.

It gave sharpshooting knuckles
and dexterous elbows.

It gave love for liminal places:
balcony, porch, driveway.

It gave meetings like catacombs.

It gave a need for vitality,
ferment: sourdough and seeds.

It gave the question—once again
who would you risk death to love?

It gave children wrapping sheets
mummy-tight, women bolting doors.

It gave a chemo port for news.

It gave a new binary: essential/non
sacrificial/work-from-home.

It gave appreciation for the veil,
blemished emotions concealed.

It gave climate change shelter:
Drought in throat, wildfire in the gut.

It gave space as latex.

It gave familiarity with curves
and words: anosmia, super-spreader.

It gave tests by blood and swab,
and the other test: transform or not.

It took delight in connecting dots,
playing six degrees of separation.

It took basketball nets and hoops.

It took holstered soft drinks, faces
flickering with the same story.

It took commencements, and clink:
chin chin, *salud*, *l'chaim*.

It took wandering in and out
of shops, fending off
salespeople with "just looking!"

It took salespeople.

It gave the stretch and snap
of a worn rubber band.

It gave robins boomier voices.

It gave an abundance of caution,
contact-free delivery.

It gave a quest for reagents,
reactants, every one of us.

It gave the common roots
of *hospital*: hostel, hospice,
inhospitable.

It gave breath as baptism on repeat.

Resilience V

> One of the core promises of
> capitalism—transformation through
> consumption—is another version of
> the promise addiction makes.
> —Leslie Jamison

Everything is a client of something. Even the birch
understands the power of the consumer (water, sun,
carbon dioxide). Nobody's victim. It never whines,
I'm sessile. Mover and shaker, it does manufacturing
—yes, I can!—AND service. The birch has a brand
like Trenton, New Jersey. It makes; the world takes.
A patient on a ventilator is a client, vaxx and spend
the only way through this crisis. The birch will
innovate its way out of any pickle; the woods are
dense with angel investors. I never intended to get
into the business, but isn't that what all dealers say?
I've got CO_2 to offload and, lucky for us, the birch
is buying. Empathy junkie with deep knowledge
of the underground economy, it's not averse to sharing
with a nearby fir. I call that waste, not monetizing
your network. Might as well be needle exchange.
The birch must not have gotten the memo: mutual aid's
moment has passed. A sucker is born every minute
in the forest. What's the greatest show on earth, if not
drought, floods, and fire. A ticket holder is a client.
Defer to the lap of popcorn, blue tongue, distracted
gaze. No clients better be harmed in the making.
We can't afford to shut down the production.

Lying Flat

Tangping (躺平) or "lying flat" was a movement begun by Chinese youth in 2021.

The young women leaned away from their desks and closed their eyes. "We don't *want* to see ourselves in five years." Tired of building their platforms, all the young people began to slump in their chairs. It dawned on them: their passions were brats in need of a time-out. Little by little, the youth slid to the floor, fell over like babies too wobbly to sit up. Supine, palms upturned, they cried in unison, "Lying flat is justice!" Never had they been so influential. Soon every office, coffee shop, crammed bedroom became a pop-up studio. Savasana in the morning, Savasana at noon, Savasana all the livelong day. "No more wolf culture," declared the youth. Stickers were distributed with the image of a possum, which many wore on their forehead. One woman was overheard saying, "I want to eat oysters on my back like an otter." This became a rallying cry for the resistance. But rather than speak aloud anymore, the youth brought their hands together over their chests: a rock in one fist and a cell phone in the other. They tapped the rock against the phone: *click, click, click*. Screens cracked but the young people did not leave their backs. Freedom wasn't ringing. Freedom was the sound of living bodies lying like clappers without bells.

Seam and Sieve

She coughs over coffee and can't swallow toast
Hospice's six-month contract was a quarantine
Without bread without mother dough's acrid smell
No one said starter must be endlessly fed

Hospice was a six-month contract we bid on
With one deliverable hurry-up and wait
Although no one said it not me not the nurse
Communicable diseases are less lonely

With one deliverable the production line
Slowed the shifts indecipherable from breaks
Her loneliness impossible to communicate
Not said *I'm serving a life sentence in bed*

COVID-slowed days indecipherable phases
That promise dilation make me impatient
As my mother serving her sentence in bed
Shut in–weary end-wary we wait or live

Labor too promised me dilation impatient
To be broken open and the world to fall in
Push-weary end-wary I waited for love
Slippery urge with a long cord for detaching

I've broken into a spinning world of cracks
Every continent divided I join with gold
Slip it between a glitter seam for attaching
One kind of waiting to another lovely scar

I wait for bread branded with black prison bars
To shoot from the old toaster startled swallows
My morning tangy and thick from life's slow strain
Sourdough gone I have yogurt's acrid smell now

Tradition Is the Prison in Which You Live

Tradition from the Latin verb for hand down, surrender, or entrust.
Its doublet (not as in Shakespeare's close-fitting jacket) is treason.
Some American traditions: pumpkin spice latte, turkey pardoning,
and plea bargaining. America, I hear you counting: two million
and ninety-four thousand behind bars. Lock-us-up! America just
like the sonnet is an inherited constraint. You can choose a form
but not the country you're born in, not your parents. A church provides
sanctuary unless you can't leave. Two cells fuse to make an embryo.
Confinement after giving birth—that's a tradition. Sometimes, love is
the prison you live in, a hard yard you circle, doing time without
ever growing older. When her mother died, my friend's sentence ended.
She surrendered her uniform and walked through the gates unguarded, numb
-erless, only an envelope under her arm: treacherous release.
No one waiting for her, no one who'll take her call, no matter the hour.

Provincetown

> AIDS obliges people to think of sex as having,
> possibly, the direst consequences: suicide. Or murder.
> —Susan Sontag

The summer I danced to Donna Summer's endless "I Feel Love,"
ecstatic, wanting to reach out, touch every peek-a-boo buttock
at the A House—that's attic, not asshole—where the men wore chaps
without pants. When I say to my daughter I'd like to go back
to P-town, do I mean the place or the time? All pandemic, we joke
about the "before times," but I have two, only one is innocent.
I tell her about the IUD I got that summer at eighteen,
—it failed—the daughter (because I can't imagine a son) who would
have been her older sister, but not about the boss from Café Blasé
living in the cabin next to ours, how each of us slept with him
between visits from his New York girlfriend, every weekend's hat
more outrageous than the last. Jean-Paul was tall and skinny, a French
cartoon, he coiled a scarf around his neck even in summer,
sported antique aviators, dark and round with side shields. Urbane,
he fed us lines, and we laughed afterward about his breasts. Fallen
pilot and his little princes. "Like lying down next to a corpse,"
we whispered. He was thirty-five. Provincetown was the place
my father went when he left my mother, me inside her, to write,
out-drink Mailer, dedicate himself to his life's work of dying
young, which he did five summers before my Donna summer.

After last call, we'd get a slice at Spiritus, grab a bottle,
head to the graveyard behind our cabin where the disco lived
on in the soft crenulated earth of our brains. We waited
for Carrie's hand to emerge, begged for something to grab us, pull us
down as the bass from "Born to Be Alive" thudded like toppling
tombstones. And on Bradford Street, the star of *Multiple Maniacs*,

Desperate Living, and *Female Trouble*, Cookie Mueller, walked by
in her mules, and the director, too, with his signature thin,
Sharpie-black mustache. We were all silent movie actors. Each night,
as I fell asleep, I reviewed the rushes. This was between
freshman and sophomore year, the summer I tunneled my way up
after seventeen years underground, proud nymph, ready to sing
my tymbalic song. Cookie died at forty. Someone's blood, semen,
did what heroin couldn't. *You will not need alcohol, you will
not have to worry about cellulite or cigarettes or cancer
or AIDS or venereal disease. You will be free*, she wrote before
dying. And wry Ivan, cheekbones like armor, his dreadlocked
scalp smelling of seaweed and asphalt. I breathed it in whenever
he gave me the chance. Older but not old. I was never sure
where he slept at night. He said he was a poet, so I forgave
his coital nod. We met on the dance floor, "Le Freak" by Chic playing.

Older now than I was then, my daughter knows time and place can't
be untwined. We'll always remember quarantine as this teal couch
dusted with northern light, facing a balcony where a crow
with one foot eats from my hand, and I feel love. We joke about
the before times, but I have two, only one is innocent. No more
falling free. How many you and me's in Summer's endless song?
Sex was just the after-party, a dim basement with no windows,
sticky floor, a few people swaying, cup in hand, not ready
to go. Ivan died at forty-one, someone's blood. From his poem
"Letter from Provincetown," *the beauty / of this place / is beyond
me*. I remember the weight of him, the sudden heaviness
mid-thrust when he would leave me. *I can never do it justice*.

Angrief

1.

Before we saw a knee take a life, become a cross worn in remembrance of him, the knee made itself into a fist. On bended knee, the football player asked for our hand. Not a fist lifted to the sky but a fist pressed against grass, gravel, granite. Digging in. When a small dog like a terrier hunts vermin—roots it out—we say it *goes to ground*. In the nine minutes and twenty-nine seconds that the police officer pressed his knee into George Floyd's neck, light traveled from the nearest star and fell on earth.

2.

Angrief kneeled, angrief chanted through masks, angrief walked the dolorous ways between office buildings, and the helicopters bore down on the procession, eyeballs without lids. We became the carcass in tall grass you locate by the buzzards. For those of us who had never known presumption of guilt, never felt its ceaseless rotor-wash, the deafening days, noisome nights were just a taste. As from an entitled spoon that hovers over, lands on, someone else's plate.

3.

Go back in time or go nowhere at all. Either way, you'll ask yourself, who am I? The upturned crowd in the face gazing at the Black body, trapeze artist without a net, or the officer who looked away, stood like a wall between two countries. Sometimes my heart is a shoe, cracked but capable of luster. Inside is a tree, the trunk a metal rod that I keep turning, turning. I stretch the leather, and still, it's tight. The Rabbi said, "You are not obligated to complete the work, but neither are you free to abandon it."

Now You Don't See It, Now You Do

"Now You Don't See It, Now You Do" is the title of Carol's talk, which begins with a photo of Jerusalem that hung in her childhood living room. Taken by her father from the Mount of Olives, it was similar to the photo of the Old City that hung in many Jewish-American homes.

*

In my dream—maybe in yours, too?—I can't get to where I want to go. I'm in a bustling train station, and no one speaks my language. No, that's not it. I've boarded a train that won't stop where I want to get off. Or is it I'm on a train that won't stop?

*

Carol shares how she and others like her would gaze at the photo, hearts swelling with pride and whatever the Hebrew is for *saudade*, without *seeing* the two most captivating, glittering, iconic even, details: the golden Dome of the Rock and the Al-Aqsa Mosque. Decades later, she can't not see them, and wonders why she never wondered: what are these Muslim holy places doing on all our Jewish walls, in what we thought of as *our Jerusalem*?

*

"Now You Don't See It, Now You Do" could easily have been the title of the Kenneth Koch poem inspired by a sign at a Kenyan railroad crossing: "One Train May Hide Another." All the poems and songs about trains could fill a Bible. What would we dream if that book sat in the bedside drawer of every motel room in America?

*

What if what you go from not seeing to seeing is something that really troubles your waters, challenges the stories that you've held as true or precious about family members, relationships, the history of your country. About your own place in all of that. Your own complicity.

*

In my teacher training, I'm told to use stories from my life. "It's what your students will remember." If only *I* could remember, or at least make some up. The advice whooshes past me on its two rails, sustaining, contained. The window-framed characters flicker by before I can grasp the plot, leaving me alone on the platform with only the smell of rain on steel and crushed peanuts beneath my heels. With only moments like cars, each one coupled to the next, a lurching gangway in between.

*

Maggie Nelson writes: "As soon as a writer starts talking about the 'human need for narrative' or the 'archaic power of storytelling,' I usually find myself wanting to bolt out of the auditorium."

I don't run from narrative; it eludes me. So, I've devised a mnemonic. Storytelling? Talk to the hand. The thumb, what makes us human (we do oppose), stands for the "I," which can, of course, be a you or a she. The index finger is the point: what the protagonist seeks. The middle finger, tall barrier, fucks everything up. The ring finger represents resolution, the equilibrium marriage is meant to provide. The pinkie finger, raised at a remove from the teacup of events, gestures delicately toward the moral.

*

After the murder of George Floyd, I realized I had very schematic, incomplete versions of things that I was sure I knew, things I thought I knew. Things like, yes, there are race issues in this country, but slavery ended in 1863 with the Emancipation Proclamation. . . . Okay, if it was sustained, then with the Civil War, slavery ended. Or, yes, there are problems, it's not perfect, but it ended. Or the south was bad; the north was much better. The north was totally different. Or civil rights were won in the Act of 1964. And again, I wasn't completely naïve. Yes, there were issues, racism persisted, but it was on the way . . .

*

Take a tragedy, a system, a movement, a moment and give it an ending. Give it a terminus in history. Build a station around it. Let it be a locomotive cathedral of steel and glass. Let it be a monument to meaning with marble statuary, a fountain, and geraniums.

*

Before I woke up, what allowed me to wake (I never leave the theater until I know how the movie ends) was a dawning: I'm on an express train hurtling past my destination, but I'll be able to get off. I'll be able, the conductor tells me, to catch a local headed back in the direction I came from. I fling back the sheets, place my feet on the floor. What was it someone told me? Plant left, then right, whispering gravity and grace? No, grace and gratitude. Today, I will retrace my steps with stealth like the woman doubled over studying the sidewalk through her one contact lens. Today I will be an anniversary. Today I will be a poem turning back to where the line began. *It takes a lot to laugh; it takes a train to cry.* What are verses but words running on parallel tracks?

If It's in the Way, It Is the Way

After getting my husband's ninety-four-year-old mother (*suegra*, a word she hates)
    over the shower wall, into the bath seat, another hurdle

awaits. I aim the handheld at her back, thighs, in-between, but the spray's
    too hot, too cold, too hot, too cold. Again. Just the right

temperature when she undressed, dropping Pull-Ups to the icy floor,
    the water is no longer. Much the way help can slide

into harm and back again. I reach for a valve (Is cold right or left?
    Why do I forget?) and urgently turn until it won't.

Then, with tiny twists, I try to dial perfection, a bank safe set to explode
    like in the movies. This constant adjusting, life

as a series of hatch marks, numbers I can't make out. Two years
    into the pandemic: we hug, faces turned away

from one another's breath. Always looking over our shoulder.
    Our mouths are covered. Still, we sing.

Resilience VI

This is how we become one with our prey. Roll in shit,
coat ourselves in sinew, flesh, whatever's left behind,
masking our scent like a dog covered in dead duck
or dirt from a nitrogen-etched outline in grass. What's
called a death ring. Stink is the whistle, the ticket
to a front-row seat, sound of webbed feet pushing away.
This is how we become one with our assassin.
Shallow our breath on the floor, cover ourselves
with blood from a friend, hiding resilient innocence.
He told my teacher "good night." This is how we become
one who lives, flinching when a door opens, a book drops,
life recomposed, a verdant tuft among the divots.

PART 4
Terminal Lucidity

Although the wind
blows terribly here,
the moonlight also leaks
between the roof planks
of this ruined house.

—Izumi Shikibu,
"Although the wind,"
translated by Jane Hirshfield

Resurrection, a Cento from My Murdered Darlings

The secret of a happy marriage, the comic said,
 remains a secret.

You stripped the bed, shaking the pillow from its case,
 and with it a scorpion.

Inside your shoes, I can't help noticing how slender
 my ankles, how long

my legs look. The root of "template"—how each of us
 began—holy wedded

with rafter, plank. Awful onement. Atonement
 sticks in the craw. Better

than forgiveness, ask for nothing at all. I say
 treaty, and you say

proliferate, our thoughts a swarm of krill. At first,
 it seemed the contagion

would bring us closer. Disaster hits a city,
 and some houses crumble.

Duct tape, the softness of hot tar, and blue tarps are
 palliative like morphine.

In a snow-covered grove, the dead tree is the one
 still clinging to its leaves.

Did we kill the scorpion right away? Examine
 it under glass awhile

before flushing? You think riddance; I think backfire.
 Like a ballerina's

upswept arm, the artful curve of the tail belying
its purpose. Culture me,

go on, make me your own. The secret to walking
the plank is a blindfold.

As Seen on TV

Ran in PJs to the mailbox with a jangly envelope of coins, no stamp: *Send sea monkeys!* Copied a judo move on Juanita, whose head hit the sidewalk. Couldn't sit still while Nadia Comaneci back-flipped across the console screen my grandmother with a broken hip cautioned would ruin my eyes, brain, if I sat too close. Nadia got three Olympic golds. I got crutches. Left off living in my mother's toile (blue and white pastoral of aproned maidens, wheelbarrows, lambs in repeat), and moved to Gilligan's Island where survival was never the question, only which shipwreck I would be. When did I stop thinking everything was possible? Fear used to be a finger curling *closer, my pretty*, hurrying me past the wooly mammoth to push through tourists, stare at shrunken heads, the Hope Diamond, bound feet. TV screens keep getting bigger and fear's circle keeps getting smaller. No one writes "return to sender" anymore. We recycle, drop the bad luck in a bin. Even if I stand absolutely still, my toes are going to cross a line.

Guns and Butter

"Pull your soldiers to your ears," says
the meditation teacher (I won't lie, I'm at war
with my body), before correcting herself.
"Shoulders!" she laughs. "Now, drop them."
We're shrugging the day away with deep
inhales and long *ahhhs* on the exhale,
preparing for surrender, when the sound
of our disarmament summons my mother.

Before the cancer in her lungs lit up
her cerebellum like rocket fire, before
she had to rest every block she walked
on someone's stoop, she started sighing,
the frequent flush of lungs as attention-
getting as an unmuted toilet on Zoom.
I took this air hunger for irritation,
resignation (the wrong kind of white flag)
folding into disposition, the way we hope
by meditating enough (there's a dose-
response) to elide state and trait.

How often do we blame the hungry? I help
myself to a bonus breath (piling seconds
on the inhale's already heaping plate)
twelve times an hour, and no one's ever
called it a handout. Because the iron lung
wouldn't let them do what even a mouse
must to survive, the first polio patients
died inside. When was the last time
you breathed a sigh of relief? Relished it
(rich as an extra pat of butter on your toast),
never realizing it was the bread itself.

The Chemistry of Distance

> Someone asked me—what's the use of a balloon?
> I replied—what's the use of a newborn baby?
> —Benjamin Franklin

1.

The Polaroid, fossil within a fossil,
walk-on-the-moon wondrous, bygone
the way a hot air balloon may never be,
is of me on my seventh birthday.

Nucleus in an atom of girls, face
upturned, I'm beaming at party balloons
—translucent orbs of blue, yellow,
red, and green—we've punched and head-
butted to the ceiling, forever out of reach
in the photo, our arms permanently
outstretched to catch. Why does this
square of stasis move me so? Arbitrary
reliquary, it inspires not devotion
but revision. The power to see again
through polychrome-tinted latex
glasses: crepe streamers, ponytails,
sugar rose dresses, smocking and tulle.

The instant in its corset glints black garnet
and jet, mourning jewelry in a velvet box.

2.

In 1783 two brothers put *a cloud
in a paper bag*, and a rooster, sheep,
and duck, the world's first aeronauts,

spent eight minutes aloft, so I have
barnyard animals to thank for this
terror on my husband's birthday
—you're only sixty once:
the ride I've arranged as a surprise.
The pilot ignites the fire overhead,
louder than a thousand bubbling bongs,
the gaping lung inhales, holds it in,
and suddenly, we're all high on the silence,
every sound—*Gary, in the house! Now!*
a dog barking, tires turning on gravel—
is a birth cry, reminding us the cord's
been cut. The fleshy green folds, horses
like beauty marks, the countable trees.
As everything tender, transient that must be
protected by us, from us—firmament
as fontanel—recedes, fear kicks in
and I drop to my knees. What do I know

about *Enduring Love*? The book begins
indelibly with an organ-splattering accident,
and I am not "intrepid Pilâtre who never
loses his head," first to fly and die
in a balloon. My husband and daughter,
hair whipping behind them heroically,
stand upright, admire the diorama below,
and laugh as I crouch on the basket floor,
praying, wiping away tears, cursing
the chattering chaser on the other end
of the pilot's cell phone, distracting him
from nearby power lines as he tries to guide
her car to wherever it is we might land.

3.

I came down gradually, and I was not hurt a bit.
But I found myself in the midst of a strange people,
who, seeing me come from the clouds, thought
I was a great wizard. Of course, I let them think so . . .

As grown-ups, it isn't Dorothy we feel for
but the balloonist from Omaha, the poseur
behind the screen even a small terrier
could topple. I can throw my voice, too.
Meet my dummies: wife, do-gooder,
poet (the pleasure is all mine), mother.
That day in the sky when my vaudeville
died, it was plain to see that all the emeralds
were only words, my only city.

Because distance is a chemical reaction.
Because adventure can be an aperture.
Because exposure must be calculated.

Was it the sky that brought out my dark
contours, scratched the emulsion
to reveal . . . ? But that isn't the instant
I want to frame. Instead, let it be this
that rises from the silty bottom,
pulls into focus, dries before our eyes,
more nostalgic than paper, silver,
"Montgolfier Gas," a brazier
for burning wet wool and straw,
or Pilâtre's torn green topcoat:

The photo not taken of the family's field,
chicken coop in a corner, the single mother

and two grown sons, one in camouflage,
and their maimed Shepherd who delivered us
from the sky, folded with us the thousand
square yards of nylon in rainbow stripes,
held our hands as we recited the balloonist's
prayer, giving thanks for our safe return,
before the chaser fetched plastic cups
from the pickup, and the pilot, holding the bottle
of champagne by its neck, launched the cork,
before it fell to earth in the effervescent dusk.

Course Correction

A time will come when you no longer lower yourself, sit on the ground comfortably, when you decide to keep your distance because to let down your guard might mean never getting up, the earth's low murmur deafening. So, you stay out of earshot. You will want nothing more than to picnic on the grass, basket of gingham friends, stoned and lolling on a blanket, blades tickling your ankles as you munch on dragonflies, slurp clouds, neither last night's rain nor dog shit impediment to a worm's eye view, glimpse of starling tongue. But worms don't have eyes and the bones that carry you carry earth, not molten but marrow at their center. You will amble upright on their axis around the park's green heart, willing another lap, the asteroid to course correct, not collide, matter with matter, lycra with dirt, flames oozing, and soot Ace-bandaging the sun, a labyrinth of underground caves forming like scars, sinkholes tunneling to lightless rivers full of blind fish, submerged signs with skull and crossbones: *Divers, enter at your own risk.*

Gold Chains and Squash Blossoms

for Ruth (1936–2011)

1.

I open my jewelry box and ask my daughter what she wants. This
is the beginning of fall, of learning to love the bare in my branches,
wind that carries away everything. The "child," no longer dependent,
asks for a chain. We dig out one of my mother's, which she deems perfect:

unknotted and slinky. I never did cling to my mother's prized
possessions—gold-rimmed china, cut crystal, my grandmother's tea set,
silverware resting in its velvet-lined casket—bequeathed to me,
her only offspring. My link to her, dead over a decade now,

is trust, a filament harder than metal, which I thread through my daughter,
a trust that I/she would figure *it* out. Keep myself busy weekend
mornings while my mother slept in, learn to tie my shoes if told not
to leave my room, disappear the food on my plate after she'd left

the table (in paper napkins behind books). If only I could wrap
myself around her, dead more than a decade, clasp that nonchalance.
I want to hang from her fearlessness, albeit circumscribed—a neck
by its necklace—to a condo the size of a ring case and shared

studio down the block (she never learned to drive). But I'm too
afraid of failure to let life unfold, always limiting myself
to what I know. She could have taught me: 18 karat rings are for melting,
precious stones for prying loose, and from all this undoing, the striking,

flawed, steadily improving takes shape. Until cancer, she was flex shaft,
soldering iron, glue gun, wire cutter, disk punch, Mod Podge, paint
roller, stained blue jeans (always wipe hands *here*), white Keds, size 5,
worn under full-length sable. How many interlocking women are we?

2.

A seed, brought by a breeze or bird, landed in a round patch of dirt
not bricked over, where two walls of my patio meet. After three weeks
away, I returned to a bristly vine as long as Jack's beanstalk
was tall, snaking down the walkway, a gourd growing every two feet.

"Cut one open," counseled a friend who cooks, "and see what kind it is."
Hard orange flesh that softened after roasting produced sweet squash soup.
Once the ripe gourds were harvested, the vine turned brown and shriveled,
as my friend had warned. What she didn't prepare me for: a new vine

sprouting at the middle and climbing—no, hurrying—up a flight
of garden stairs, as if the body on its deathbed could dissolve headfirst,
followed by neck, shoulders, and chest before extruding from its navel
a muscly green arm, raised in the air, reaching. The descendant ascending.

My mother's tools, Lenox, books, and Waterford long since donated
or sold, I've kept only what I need. The jewelry she bought and made,
her ink sketches, a drawerful of photos, and her fur, cut and sheared
to line my winter coat. Worn on the inside where only I know it's there.

Wind in a Box

The landlady in black knocked, gesturing wildly. *Anemos*, she cried.
Anemos! It had been a sleepless night of wind and neither of us
spoke Greek. Spirits? we hazarded. Ghosts? How did Latin for enliven
turn into anger? May your animus be brief! I wish I could be
amicable, but civility is built on form, form on what is
predictable. The doorstep's box will be ripped open, the packer's breath
released, the cardboard flattened, tied, and trashed. Another order fulfilled.
The ancients said we contain earth, fire, water, and air. Terrance Hayes said
the sonnet is wind in a box. On the highway, the wind urges me
into an oncoming trailer the way I fight the tongue's urge to swerve
into the dentist's drill. Nine months in a windless box, and every breeze
freaks out my newborn, eyes squeezed tight. How to keep a ghost from
finding you,
finding this body—a spare room in an island house that lets air move
through as it hugs rock. Kneel down and hold your hand to the threshold.
Feel it.

Final Descent

After my mother died, I spent sunsets on the roof, scouring the clouds, white tea leaves in a drained and darkening cup. A few times, I thought I sensed her up there, lingering like the smell of her empty apartment: old paperbacks, tobacco, and *Miss Dior*. At once, a disembodied ear and the domed auditorium. How must it feel to be perpetually traversed by smooth-talking planes, satellites that repeat the same old stories? I have no religion, and still I'm a sucker for ascent. And yet, the sky is not the only vastness. *Listen, O Drop, give yourself up without regret / and in exchange gain the Ocean.* Why not a candle lit by other candles in a cathedral of roots, or an orange blossom in the Alhambra of my heart? Call it failure of imagination, a reflexive craning toward the light. On top of our house by the airport, tracking a jet's descent, I imagine the passengers rehearsing for touchdown: what not to forget, who to call first, the psychic unbuckling. Another day that the door with glowing red letters did not open.

The night she died, she called to say she couldn't breathe. I had just left her bedside, after checking the plastic nozzles in her nose and kissing her good night. "I'm dying," said the voice on the phone. "If you're able to talk to me, you're still breathing," I laughed. And with that, she laughed, too, her oxygen sliding down like a window shade before a long flight. Undimmed, immune to the sleeping pill's effects, she was more herself than she'd been in months. "Terminal lucidity," they call it.

Resilience VII

When my husband, breaching a border, braving the virus,
finally came home again, my crow ghosted me: a flung
fling. Or was he the ambulance that quietly vanishes,
vitals restored? Two weeks went by before the bird
returned to my railing, skittish phantom, head
like a shaved pubis. Had he been attacked?
Envied for his access to endless kibble?
Picked on due to disability?
Each time I saw him,
he looked worse
and I knew.
I knew the
shape of
this curve.
Until I didn't,
and he started sloping
toward—there is no other word—
resplendence. Not dying but molting.

Acknowledgments

Thank you to the editors of the following publications in which these poems/essays first appeared, sometimes with different titles.

32 Poems: "After the Ecstasy, the Laundry" and "Tradition Is the Prison in Which You Live"

Baltimore Review: "The Chemistry of Distance"

Barrow Street: "Resilience I"

Birdcoat Quarterly: "Course Correction"

The Citron Review: "Slogan 34: Don't Transfer the Ox's Load to the Cow"

Conduit: "Slogan 38: Don't Seek Others' Pain as the Limbs of Your Own Happiness"

Crab Creek Review: "Resurrection, a Cento from My Murdered Darlings"

Diode: "Slogan 25: Don't Talk about Injured Limbs"

DMQ Review: "Free Trade Agreement"

Jet Fuel Review: "Taking Dictation"

Gargoyle: "Resilience IV" and "Resilience VII"

Indianapolis Review: "Resilience II"

MER: "Final Descent"

Pangyrus: "Resilience III"

On the Seawall: "Resilience V" and "Lying Flat"

Salamander: "Regard the Other as a Verb" and "Provincetown"

Southern Humanities Review: "Home Improvement"

The Superstition Review: "If It's in the Way, It Is the Way"

SWWIM: "Love It or List It"

Unbroken, Prose Poems: "The Lounge Chair Does the Work"

The Westchester Review: "Wind in a Box" and "Slogan 27: Work with the Greatest Defilements First."

"After the Ecstasy, the Laundry" appeared in *Best American Poetry 2024*.

"Resilience III" was included in the anthology, *Where We Dwell*, Pangyrus 10, 2023, as "Resilience I."

And gratitude to—

My family: Mario Bravo, Amaya Bravo-France, Mariah Walker, Ron Brendle, Theresa Bolinger, Rebecca Maybee, all the still-to-be-met/discovered offspring of Bill Walker, and the Deprez family.

My hometown: Washington to some, D.C. to me. The writing of *Locomotive Cathedral* was supported in part by the D.C. Commission on the Arts and Humanities, which receives support from the National Endowment for the Arts.

The Virginia Center for Creative Arts and the Hermitage Artist Retreat, where some of these poems were written and revised.

Hilda Raz for awarding *Locomotive Cathedral* the Backwaters Prize in Poetry Honorable Mention, and to all the amazing editorial and production staff at the University of Nebraska, especially Courtney Ochsner and Tayler Lord but also Terry Boldan, Tish Fobben, Lacey Losh, Leif Milliken, and Kayla Moslander.

Mary Jo Salter, who selected "After the Ecstasy, the Laundry" for inclusion in *Best American Poetry 2024*.

Diane Seuss, whose poems and generosity to the poetry community have been an inspiration.

Rage Hezekiah and Michael Bazzett for their support and poetry kinship.

My Warren Wilson MFA posse, the LS Pretzels: Subhaga Crystal Bacon, Jennifer Martelli, and Barbara O'Dair. We saved each other during the pandemic and will continue to "fix" poems through the next one. I am because you are.

Sandra Beasley, who saw my poems and helped me do the same, and Susan Rich for her close reading.

All the poet-moms (you know who you are!), but especially Marcela Sulak, Sarah Rose Nordgren, Martha Silano, Anna V. Q. Ross, Cin Salach, Lisa Ampleman, and Backwaters Press mates Julie Choffel and Jennifer K. Sweeney.

Jennifer Clement for inspiring me to write my first lyric essay and revealing to me how prose and poetry can cohabitate, shack up, have a thing going on.

Naomi Shihab Nye for the many poems she's written that teach compassion better than I ever could, and for sharing my poem "What It Took and What It Gave" at San Francisco's Zen hospice center during the height of the pandemic.

Washington Writers Publishing House, the oldest collective press in the country that's been supporting writers in "the DMV" since 1975, for publishing my first book of poems, *Provenance*.

Katerina Stoykova of Accents Publishing and Diode editor/publisher Patty Paine for awarding *Mother, Loose* Judge's Choice.

Stanford University's Center for Compassion and Altruism Research and Education, the Compassion Institute, and all my Compassion Cultivation Training teachers and colleagues, with a deep bow to Thupten Jinpa, Leah Weiss, Kelly McGonigal, Erika Rosenberg, Margaret Cullen, Robert Cusick, Miroo Kim, Maria Paula Jimenez, Tori Higa-Sarris, Kathleen Ledoux, and most of all to Laura Banks, who mentored me when I began teaching and from whom I learn so much.

Downtown Dharma in Washington D.C. Everyone should be lucky enough to have such a spiritual home with teachers past and present like Devin Maroney, Kristin Barker, and Travis Spencer. Sending *metta* to the DD community, but especially to Nick Menzies and Vince Lampone.

Everyone in my 2016 DCI cohort at Stanford. "It's more than a year!"

And last but not least, my muse, René, who became something of a celebrity at my D.C. condominium.

Notes

"**After the Ecstasy, the Laundry**" is also the title of a book by Jack Kornfield published in 2001.

"**Free Trade Agreement, a *Zuihitsu***": Mexican president Porfirio Diaz said, "Poor Mexico, so far from God and so close to the U.S." Antoine Lavoisier, founder of modern chemistry, pronounced, "Nothing is lost, nothing is created, everything is transformed."

"**Women Talking**" takes its title from a movie directed by Sarah Polley, based on the book by Miriam Toews. The poem is dedicated to my friends Subhaga Crystal Bacon and Jennifer Martelli.

"**Love It or List It**": "Every criticism, judgment, diagnosis, expression of anger is the tragic expression of an unmet need" is from Marshall Rosenberg, *Nonviolent Communication: A Language of Life*.

"**People of the Dog**": "*Para el mexicano la vida es una posibilidad de chingar o de ser chingado*" comes from Octavio Paz's *Labyrinth of Solitude and Other Writings*.

"**Resilience II**": "Something there is that doesn't love a wall" is from Robert Frost's "Mending Wall."

"**You're Like a Dull Knife**": In the song "Talkin' Loud, Sayin' Nothing," James Brown sings, "Like a dull knife / just ain't cutting."

"**Taking Dictation**": "You're one of my five real friends" allegedly appears in a letter written by Vladimir Putin to former Italian prime minister Silvio Berlusconi. In 1972, President Mobutu of the Democratic Republic of Congo (then Zaire) renamed himself Mobutu Sese Seko Nkuku Ngbendu Wa Za Banga, which translates as "The all-powerful warrior who, because of his endurance and inflexible will to win, goes from conquest to conquest, leaving fire in his wake." Donald Trump, in a 2005 hot mic recording released in 2016, said, "I'm automatically attracted to beautiful women—I just start kissing them, it's like a magnet. Just kiss. I don't even wait. And when you're a star, they let you do it. You can do anything."

"Home Improvement": "When we are observing love, we are that love" is from Guy Armstrong's *Emptiness: A Practical Guide for Meditators*.

"It's a Joy to Be Hidden and a Disaster Not to Be Found": Pediatrician and analyst D. W. Winnicott wrote this in his 1965 book *The Maturational Processes and the Facilitating Environment: Studies in the Theory of Emotional Development*.

"Slogan 7": "*Tonglen*" refers to the Tibetan Buddhist meditation practice. It involves taking in suffering on the inhale and giving its antidote on the exhale. It's also referred to as an exchange of self with other.

"Slogan 8": "To our senses, things offer only their rejections" is from the poem "Of Colors," by Paul Valéry.

"Slogan 49": The phrase "mix their flour at night with broken glass" comes from the Tom Lux poem "The People of the Other Village." The first line of the poem, continuing from the title, is, "hate the people of this village."

"Slogan 59": Shane McCrae's words and ideas about confessional poetry come from Episode 111 of the podcast *Commonplace: Conversations with Poets (and Other People)*, hosted by Rachel Zucker and aired on May 16, 2023. In the podcast, she reads from McCrae's email to her. The final line of the poem refers to a COVID pandemic performance that took place at Barcelona's opera house when it reopened on June 20, 2020. A string quartet performed for an audience composed entirely of potted plants.

"**Slogan 4**" is indebted to Heather McGhee's book *The Sum of Us: What Racism Costs Everyone and How We Can Prosper Together*.

"**Resilience V**": The Leslie Jamison quote is from her 2018 book *The Recovering: Intoxication and its Aftermath*.

"**Tradition Is the Prison in Which You Live**": This poem is dedicated to my friend Victoria Godfrey. Marcel Duchamps uttered this sentence in a 1964 interview with Calvin Tomkins. John Murillo said during a panel discussion at the 2022 Association of Writers and Writing Programs conference in Philadelphia that "America is an inherited constraint."

"**Provincetown**": The quotes from Cookie Mueller, the star of many of John Waters's movies, are from her posthumously published book, *Ask Dr. Mueller: The Writings of Cookie Mueller*, High Risk Books, 1997. The lines of the poem "Letter from Provincetown" are by Ivan Wendell Hubbard. The poem is posted in its entirety at https://oddballmagazine.com/retraction-memorable-times-with-ivan/.

"**Now You Don't See It, Now You Do**": This essay is dedicated to my friend of many years, Carol Bardenstein. The Maggie Nelson quote can be found in her book *The Red Parts*. "It Takes a Lot to Laugh, It Takes a Train to Cry" is a song by Bob Dylan.

"**Resilience VI**": "He told my teacher 'good night'" are the words of Miah Cerillo, an eleven-year-old survivor of the Uvalde massacre in 2022.

"**Resurrection, a Cento from My Murdered Darlings**": This cento is comprised of lines taken from poems of mine I've given up on, abandoned.

"**The Chemistry of Distance**": the Montgolfier brothers described the first hot air balloon flight as like "putting a cloud in a paper bag." The brothers mistakenly thought that they had discovered a new gas ("Montgolfier gas"), lighter than air, when all they had done was heat it, making it less dense and lighter than the surrounding air. One of two men to first experience flight in a hot air balloon, Pilâtre de Rozier came to be known as "Intrepid Pilâtre who never loses his head." The passage beginning, "I came down gradually, and I was not hurt a bit" is from L. Frank Baum's *The Wonderful Wizard of Oz*.

"Wind in a Box": Terrance Hayes, author of *Wind in a Box* (2006), said about the sonnet in a 2018 *Rumpus* interview, "The form has felt like that: wind in a box."

"Final Descent": "Listen, O Drop, give yourself up without regret / and in exchange gain the Ocean" is from a poem by Rumi (*Mathnawi* IV, 2619–22, *Jewels of Remembrance*, trans. Kabir & Camille Helminski).

Backwaters Prize in Poetry

2023 Julie Choffel, *Dear Wallace*
   Honorable Mention: Brandel Franco de Bravo, *Locomotive Cathedral*
2022 Laura Reece Hogan, *Butterfly Nebula*
   Honorable Mention: Henrietta Goodman, *Antillia*
2021 Laura Bylenok, *Living Room*
   Honorable Mention: Sophie Klahr, *Two Open Doors in a Field*
2020 Nathaniel Perry, *Long Rules: An Essay in Verse*
   Honorable Mention: Amy Haddad, *An Otherwise Healthy Woman*
2019 Jennifer K. Sweeney, *Foxlogic, Fireweed*
   Honorable Mention: Indigo Moor, *Everybody's Jonesin' for Something*
2018 John Sibley Williams, *Skin Memory*
2017 Benjamín Naka-Hasebe Kingsley, *Not Your Mama's Melting Pot*
2016 Mary Jo Thompson, *Stunt Heart*
2015 Kim Garcia, *DRONE*
2014 Katharine Whitcomb, *The Daughter's Almanac*
2013 Zeina Hashem Beck, *To Live in Autumn*
2012 Susan Elbe, *The Map of What Happened*
2004 Aaron Anstett, *No Accident*
2003 Michelle Gillett, *Blinding the Goldfinches*
2002 Ginny MacKenzie, *Skipstone*

2001   Susan Firer, *The Laugh We Make When We Fall*

2000   David Staudt, *The Gifts and the Thefts*

1999   Sally Allen McNall, *Rescue*

1998   Kevin Griffith, *Paradise Refunded*

The Backwaters Prize in Poetry was suspended from 2005 to 2011.

To order or obtain more information on these or other University of Nebraska Press titles, visit nebraskapress.unl.edu.

www.ingramcontent.com/pod-product-compliance
Lightning Source LLC
Chambersburg PA
CBHW020012260325
24098CB00006B/110